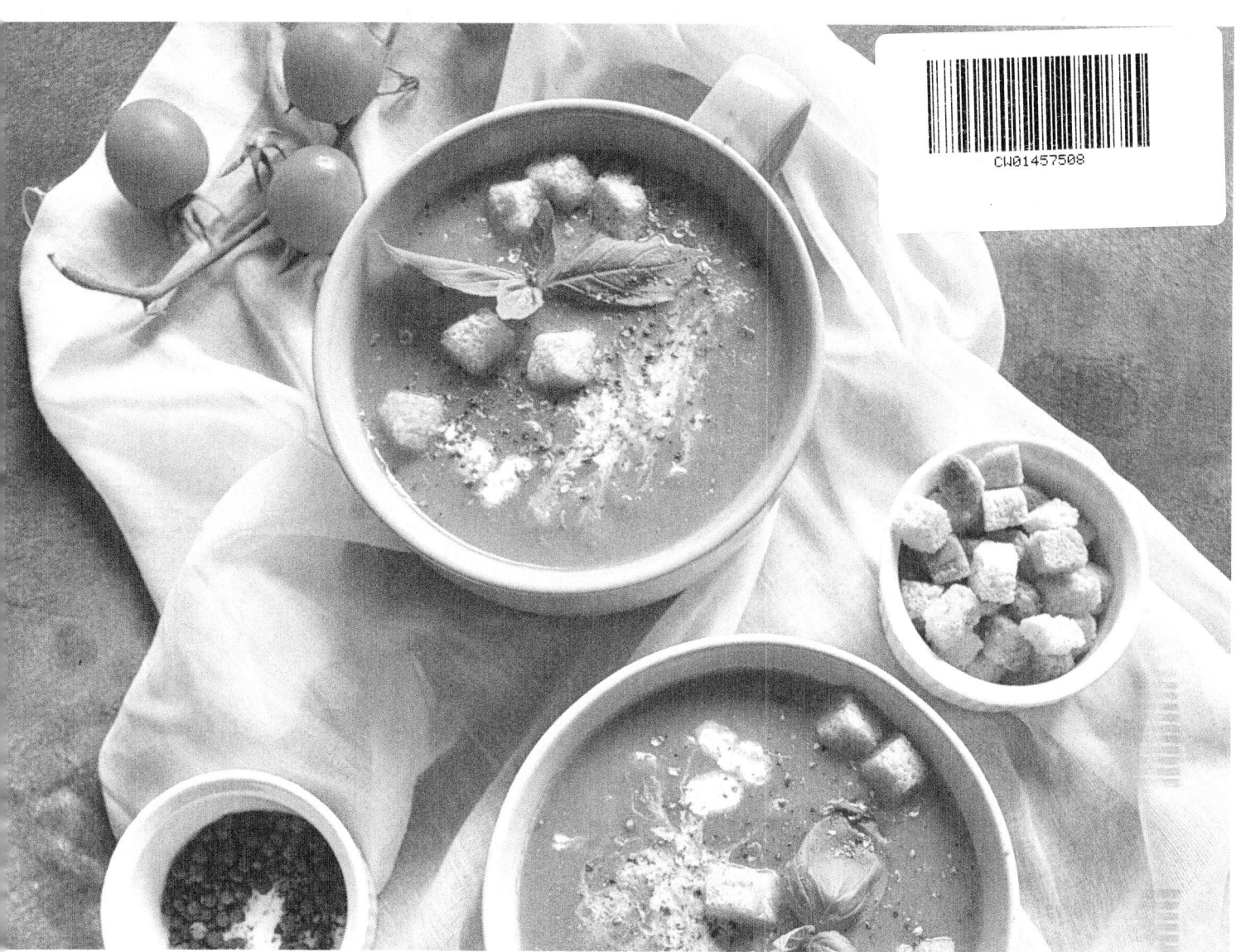

Introduction

Is there anything better on a chilly night than a piping hot bowl of soup?

A soup maker makes soup preparation much easier. You can easily add your ingredients, set soup cycle, and forget it until it's ready, freeing you up to do other important tasks while your meal cooks.

This recipe book is filled with useful information and step-by-step instructions to help you learn how to use your soup maker with ease; you'll be making soup maker recipes like a pro in no time!

How Does a Soup Maker Work?

A soup maker is an all-in-one appliance that combine multiple blending functions to make your soup chunky or smooth (or just how you like it), as well as a heating element or friction blades to cook a batch of soup in 20 to 30 minutes. Soup makers are commonly shaped like blenders or kettles.

"Regardless of whether you use a kettle or blender style soup maker, it will be able to cook soups quickly and blend soups when desired."

How to Use a Soup Maker

Step 1

Chop the Ingredients Into Small size bite pieced

- First, you'll want to start by cutting your ingredients into small pieces. Try to make all the ingredients as uniform in size as possible.

Step 2

Sauté the Ingredients:

- Sautéing vegetables and meats can help release flavor, but this is not necessary. Some soup makers have a Sautéing function that allows you to Sauté vegetables and meat at the bottom of the soup maker . If your soup maker does not have this feature, you will have to use a separate frying pan.

Step 3

Add the Ingredients to Your Soup Maker:

- Add ingredients and Stock to the Soup Maker.
- Close the Lid and Select smooth or chunky function.
- When cooking cycle is complete, open lid and adjust the seasoning
- Serve and Enjoy.

TIPS WHEN USING YOUR SOUP MAKER

1 **Gather and prepare your ingredients:**

Read through recipe you intend to make and gather all of the necessary ingredients.

2 **Start with a hot liquid:**

When you add your stock or water to the soup maker, it must be hot; otherwise, you will be adding unnecessary time to the process.

3 **Cut vegetables in small size:**

When you're adding your vegetables to the soup maker, make sure they're all cut into bite-sized pieces.This will result in an evenly 'chunky' soup, and all of vegetables will be cooked.

4 **Brown/sauté the meat:**

If you are adding meat to your soup, make sure that it is browned/sautéd so that its partially cooked.

5 **Leave the lid on:**

Do Not open the slow cooker lid during cooking process to check on your soup while it is cooking

HOW TO STORE SOUPS

1. Refrigerating Soups

If you plan to use the soup within a few days, The simplest way to store soups is to place it in a container with a tight-fitting lid and place it in the fridge for up to 3 days.

t's best to let it cool completely before storing, but don't worry if the soup is still warm; refrigerators will quickly bring it down to a safe temperature.

When you're ready to reheat the soup, simply heat it gently in a pan on the hop, microwave or in your soup maker if it contains reheat function.

2. Freezing Soups

Soups that are frozen have a much longer shelf life than those that are kept in the fridge. Soups can be safely stored in the freezer for up to three months if properly stored.

The main issue with freezing soups is quality, which is related to the soup's specific ingredients. Pasta and noodles, milk, cream, cheese, and other dairy products, rice, and potatoes are all problematic in the freezer for a variety of reasons.

Starchy ingredients like pasta, rice, and potatoes absorb too much liquid from the soup, turning it mushy. Dairy products are prone to separation. This is not to say that you can't safely freeze soups with these ingredients; just know that they won't freeze as well as soups without them. In general, the less time items spend in the freezer, the better. So, when making soups with these problematic ingredients, consider using them within weeks rather than months.

When you're ready to eat it, take it out of the freezer and let it defrost completely before reheating it in one of the methods discussed above. It will keep in the freezer for 4 to 6 months.

INDEX

VEGETABLE SOUPS

MEAT & POULTRY SOUPS

SEAFOOD SOUPS

1

Vegetable Soups

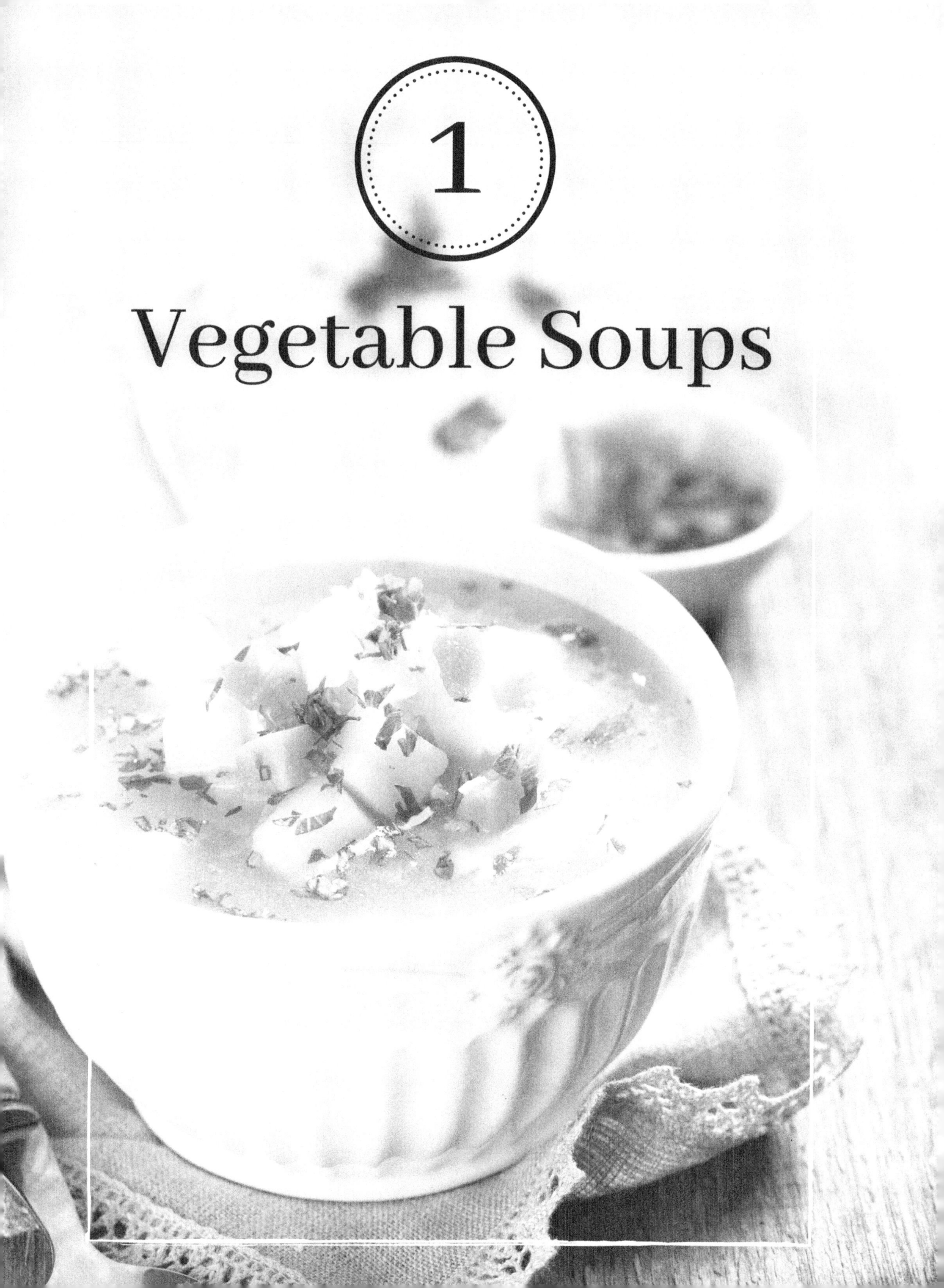

CELERY SOUP

Serves : 4   **Cook Time : 21 Mins**

Ingredients

- 400g celery, chopped
- 1 onion, chopped
- 2 garlic cloves, minced
- 500ml hot vegetable stock
- Salt & pepper to taste
- 4 tbsp double cream

Preparation Steps

1. Add all ingredients (except double cream)to the soup maker. Don't fill the soup maker above the MAX fill line or below the MIN line. Add more stock if needed.
2. Select the 'smooth soup' function.
3. Once the cycle is complete, add double cream, season with salt & pepper and stir. Transfer into bowls, then serve.

PEA SOUP

Serves : 4   Cook Time : 21 Mins

Ingredients

- 350g fresh or frozen peas
- 4 garlic cloves, minced
- 500ml hot vegetable stock
- Salt & pepper to taste

Preparation Steps

1. Add all ingredients to the soup maker. Don't fill the soup maker above the MAX fill line or below the MIN line. Add more stock if needed.

2. Select the 'smooth soup' function.

3. Once the cycle is complete, season with salt & pepper and stir. Transfer into bowls, then serve.

ASPARAGUS & CAULIFLOWER SOUP

Serves : 3   **Cook Time : 21 Mins**

Ingredients

- 500ml chicken/hot vegetable stock
- 250g cauliflower florets, chopped
- 250g asparagus, chopped
- 125g grated Old Winchester cheese
- Salt & pepper to taste

Preparation Steps

1. Add all ingredients to the soup maker. Don't fill the soup maker above the MAX fill line or below the MIN line. Add more stock if needed.
2. Select the 'smooth soup' function.
3. Once the cycle is complete, season with salt & pepper and stir. Transfer into bowls, then serve.

COURGETTE SOUP

Serves : 4   **Cook Time : 21 Mins**

Ingredients

- 3 courgettes , chopped
- 1 onion, chopped
- 2 garlic cloves, minced
- 500ml chicken or hot vegetable stock
- 4 tbsp cream cheese
- Salt & pepper to taste
- 1 tbsp lemon juice

Preparation Steps

1. Add all ingredients (except lemon juice) to the soup maker. Don't fill the soup maker above the MAX fill line or below the MIN line. Add more stock if needed.
2. Select the 'smooth soup' function.
3. Once the cycle is complete, add lemon juice, season with salt & pepper and stir. Transfer into bowls, then serve.

BROCCOLI SOUP

Serves : 4   Cook Time : 21 Mins

Ingredients

- 400ml hot vegetable stock
- 500g broccoli florets
- 225g grated cheddar cheese
- 120ml double cream
- Salt & pepper to taste

Preparation Steps

1. Add all ingredients (except cheddar cheese and double cream) to the soup maker. Don't fill the soup maker above the MAX fill line or below the MIN line. Add more stock if needed.
2. Select the 'smooth soup' function.
3. Once the cycle is complete, add cheddar cheese and double cream, season with salt & pepper and stir. Transfer into bowls, then serve.

MUSHROOM SOUP

Serves : 4   **Cook Time : 30 Mins**

Ingredients

- 1 tbsp butter
- 1 scallion, chopped
- 1 garlic clove , minced
- 300g fresh mushrooms, sliced
- 1 tsp dried oregano
- 600ml hot vegetable or hot chicken stock
- 120ml double cream
- Salt & pepper to taste

Preparation Steps

1. In a frying pan or in soup maker, heat butter and sauté the scallion, and garlic, until soft & fragrant. Add the mushrooms and sauté for 6 mins.
2. Add all ingredients (except double cream) to the soup maker. Don't fill the soup maker above the MAX fill line or below the MIN line. Add more stock if needed.
3. Select the 'smooth soup' function.
4. Once the cycle is complete, add double cream, season with salt & pepper and stir. Transfer into bowls, then serve.

SPICED PUMPKIN SOUP

Serves : 4   **Cook Time : 21 Mins**

Ingredients

- 1 kg pumpkin, cut into small pieces
- 1tbsp garam masala
- 2 tsp ground coriander
- 2 tsp ground cumin
- 1tsp chilli powder
- 3 tbsp oil
- Salt & pepper to taste

- 1 onion, chopped
- 1 tbsp ground ginger
- 2 garlic cloves, minced
- 800ml hot vegetable stock
- 120ml double cream

Preparation Steps

1. Add all ingredients (except double cream) to the soup maker. Don't fill the soup maker above the MAX fill line or below the MIN line. Add more stock if needed.
2. Select the 'smooth soup' function.
3. Once the cycle is complete, add double cream, season with salt & pepper and stir. Transfer into bowls, then serve.

CREAMY CARROT SOUP

🥣 **Serves : 4** 🕐 **Cook Time : 30 Mins**

Ingredients

- 1½ tbsp oil
- 1 onion, chopped
- 1 celery stalk, chopped
- 3 garlic cloves, minced
- 1 kg carrots, sliced
- 1.5 litre hot chicken stock
- Salt & pepper to taste

Preparation Steps

1. In a frying pan or in soup maker, heat oil and sauté the onion, and garlic, until soft & fragrant. Add the carrots and sauté for 6 mins.

2. Add all ingredients to the soup maker. Don't fill the soup maker above the MAX fill line or below the MIN line. Add more stock if needed.

3. Select the 'smooth soup' function.

4. Once the cycle is complete, season with salt & pepper and stir. Transfer into bowls, then serve.

YELLOW SPLIT PEA SOUP

Serves : 4   Cook Time : 21 Mins

Ingredients

- 250g dried yellow split peas, soaked for at least 2 hours
- 1 onion, chopped
- 1 leek, chopped
- 1 carrot, chopped
- 1 parsnip, peeled and chopped
- 1 litre hot vegetable stock
- Salt & pepper to taste

Preparation Steps

1. Add all ingredients to the soup maker. Don't fill the soup maker above the MAX fill line or below the MIN line. Add more stock if needed.
2. Select the 'smooth soup' function.
3. Once the cycle is complete, season with salt & pepper and stir. Transfer into bowls, then serve.

SYNFREE SCOTCH BROTH

🥣 **Serves : 4**   🕐 **Cook Time : 50 Mins**

Ingredients

- 2 celery stalks, chopped
- 1 onion, chopped
- 2 carrots, peeled & chopped
- 400g tinned crushed tomatoes
- 1 garlic clove, minced
- 100g raw pearl barley
- 1200ml hot vegetable stock
- 100g spring greens
- 100g frozen peas
- Salt & pepper to taste

Preparation Steps

1. Boil the raw pearl barley in a pan of hot water for 25 minutes, drain and set aside
2. Add all ingredients to the soup maker. Don't fill the soup maker above the MAX fill line or below the min line. Add more stock if needed.
3. Select the 'chunky soup' function.
4. Once the cycle is complete, season with salt & pepper and stir.
5. Transfer into bowls, then serve.

CABBAGE SOUP

Serves : 4   Cook Time :30 Mins

Ingredients

- 500g cabbage, shredded
- 1 onion, chopped
- 1 carrot, chopped
- 3 garlic cloves , minced
- 1/4 tsp of each (Oregano, Rosemary, Thyme)
- 700ml chicken or vegetable stock
- Salt & pepper to taste

Preparation Steps

1. Add all the ingredients to the soup maker and stir well. Don't fill the soup maker above the MAX fill line or below the MIN line. Add more stock if needed.
2. Set on 'chunky soup' function .
3. Once the cycle is complete, season with salt & pepper, add cream and stir. Transfer into bowls, and serve.

CARROT SOUP

Serves : 4   **Cook Time : 26 Mins**

Ingredients

- 1 tbsp butter/oil
- 1 onion, chopped
- 1 bell pepper, seeded & chopped
- 3 garlic clove , minced
- 1 tbsp turmeric powder
- 1 tsp grated fresh ginger

- 3 carrots, peeled & chopped
- 500ml hot vegetable stock
- 1 tbsp lemon juice
- Salt & pepper to taste

Preparation Steps

1. In a frying pan or in soup maker, heat butter/oil and sauté the onion, and pepper, until soft & fragrant.
2. Add all the ingredients to the soup maker and stir well. Don't fill the soup maker above the MAX fill line or below the min line. Add more water if needed.
3. Select the 'smooth soup' function.
4. Once the cycle is complete, season with salt & pepper and stir.
5. Transfer into bowls, then serve.

TURNIP SOUP

Serves : 3   **Cook Time : 33 Mins**

Ingredients

- 2 tbsp oil
- 1 onion, chopped
- 450g turnips, peeled and cubed
- ½ tsp rosemary
- 700ml hot vegetable stock
- Salt & pepper to taste

Preparation Steps

1. In a frying pan or in your soup maker, sauté the onions until soft. Add turnips, rosemary and sauté for 8 minutes, stirring frequently.

2. Add all the ingredients to the soup maker. Don't fill the soup maker above the MAX fill line or below the min line. Add more stock if needed.

3. Set on 'smooth soup' function.

4. Once the cycle is complete, season with salt & pepper, stir and transfer into bowls, then serve.

SQUASH SOUP

Serves : 3   Cook Time : 31 Mins

Ingredients

- 500g butternut squash, peeled & cubed
- 1 tbsp oil
- 1 onion, chopped
- 1 garlic clove, minced
- 400ml hot chicken stock
- 200ml milk
- Salt & pepper to taste

Preparation Steps

1. In a frying pan or in your soup maker, saute the onions and garlic, until fragrant.
2. Add all the ingredients to the soup maker. Don't fill the soup maker above the MAX fill line or below the min line. Add more stock if needed.
3. Set on 'smooth soup' function.
4. Once the cycle is complete, season with salt & pepper, stir and transfer into bowls, then serve.

BROCCOLI & STILTON SOUP

Serves : 4   Cook Time : 28 Mins

Ingredients

- 1 tbsp oil
- 450g broccoli florets
- 100g crumbled Stilton cheese
- 1 onion, chopped
- 100g leek, sliced
- 1 celery stalk, chopped
- 1 potato, peeled & chopped
- 700ml hot vegetable stock
- 2 tsp dried thyme
- Salt & pepper to taste

Preparation Steps

1. In a frying pan or in your soup maker, sauté the onions and garlic, until fragrant.
2. Add all ingredients (except cheese) to the soup maker. Don't fill the soup maker above the MAX fill line or below the min line. Add more stock if needed.
3. Set on 'smooth soup' function.
4. Once the cycle is complete, season with salt & pepper, add crumbled cheese, stir and transfer into bowls, then serve.

CHEESE & ONION SOUP

Serves : 4   Cook Time : 30 Mins

Ingredients

- 1 tbsp oil
- 1 garlic clove, minced
- 300g potato, peeled & chopped
- 600g scallions, heads trimmed and roughly chopped
- 1 tsp of dried thyme
- Salt & pepper to taste
- 800ml chicken or hot vegetable stock
- 100g grated cheddar cheese

Preparation Steps

1. In a frying pan or in the soup maker, heat oil, sauté the onions, potato and garlic for 6 mins.

2. Add all ingredients (except cheese) to the soup maker. Don't fill the soup maker above the MAX fill line or below the min line. Add more stock if needed.

3. Set on 'smooth soup' function.

4. Once the cycle is complete, season with salt & pepper, add crumbled cheese, stir and transfer into bowls, then serve.

COURGETTE & CHEESE SOUP

Serves : 4   **Cook Time : 21 Mins**

Ingredients

- 700g courgettes, chopped
- 200g potato, chopped
- 1 small onion, sliced
- 700ml hot chicken stock
- 2 tsp smoked paprika

- 100g grated cheddar cheese
- Salt & pepper to taste

Preparation Steps

1. Add all ingredients (except cheese) to the soup maker. Don't fill the soup maker above the MAX fill line or below the min line. Add more stock if needed.
2. Set on 'smooth soup' function.
3. Once the cycle is complete, season with salt & pepper, add crumbled cheese, stir and transfer into bowls, then serve.

KALE, CHEESE & BREAD SOUP

🍲 **Serves : 4**   🕐 **Cook Time : 30 Mins**

Ingredients

- 1 tbsp oil
- 200g curly kale
- 1 1/2 litre hot chicken stockpots
- 3 large garlic clove, minced
- 1 tsp grated fresh ginger
- 1 large onion, chopped

- 1 large onion, chopped
- 50g grated cheddar cheese
- 120g bread cubes, toasted
- Salt & pepper to taste

Preparation Steps

1. Add all ingredients (except bread and cheese) to the soup maker. Don't fill the soup maker above the MAX fill line or below the min line. Add more stock if needed.
2. Set on 'chunky soup' function.
3. Once the cycle is complete, season with salt & pepper, add cheese, bread cubes, stir and transfer into bowls, then serve.

CREAMY SPICED PARSNIP SOUP

☒ **Serves : 4**   🕐 **Cook Time : 25 Mins**

Ingredients

- 1 tbsp oil
- 550g parsnips, peeled & chopped
- 1 potato, peeled and chopped
- 1 onion, chopped
- 1 celery stalk, chopped
- 2 garlic cloves, chopped
- 1/2 tsp turmeric
- 1 tsp cumin seeds
- 700ml hot vegetable stock
- 150ml milk
- Salt & pepper to taste

Preparation Steps

1. In a frying pan or in the soup maker, heat oil and sauté the onions and garlic, until fragrant.
2. Add all ingredients to the soup maker. Don't fill the soup maker above the MAX fill line or below the min line. Add more stock if needed.
3. Set on 'smooth soup' function.
4. Once the cycle is complete, season with salt & pepper, stir and transfer into bowls, then serve.

PEPPER & QUINOA SOUP

Serves : 4   Cook Time : 30 Mins

Ingredients

- 1 red pepper, deseeded & chopped
- 1 yellow pepper, deseeded & chopped
- 1 green pepper, deseeded & chopped
- 2 onions, chopped
- 1 garlic clove, minced
- 1 litre hot chicken stock
- 1 1/2 tsp turmeric
- 1 1/2 tsp ginger
- 1/2 tsp coriander
- 60g quinoa
- Salt & pepper to taste

Preparation Steps

1. Add all the ingredients to the soup maker and stir. Don't fill the soup maker above the MAX fill line or below the min line. Add more stock if needed.
2. Set on 'chunky soup' function.
3. Once the cycle is complete, season with salt & pepper, stir and transfer into bowls, then serve.

BROCCOLI & PEPPER SOUP

Serves : 4   **Cook Time : 28 Mins**

Ingredients

- 1 tbsp oil
- 1 broccoli head, cut into florets
- 2 garlic cloves, minced
- 3 different colours bell peppers peppers, deseeded & chopped
- 2 celery stalks, chopped
- 3 onion, chopped

- 1 tsp ground turmeric
- 1 tsp Worcestershire sauce
- 800ml hot chicken stock
- 50ml double cream
- Salt & pepper to taste

Preparation Steps

1. In a frying pan or in the soup maker, heat oil and sauté the onions, and celery until soft.
2. Add all the ingredients (except the double cream) to the soup maker and stir. Don't fill the soup maker above the MAX fill line or below the min line. Add more stock if needed.
3. Select the 'smooth soup' function.
4. Once the cycle is complete, add double cream, season with salt & pepper. Transfer into bowls, then serve.

TOMATO & BASIL SOUP

Serves : 4   Cook Time : 21 Mins

Ingredients

- 3 shallots, chopped
- 4 garlic cloves, crushed
- 5 tomatoes, chopped
- 1 potato, peeled & chopped
- 8 basil leaves, chopped

- 1 carrot, peeled and chopped
- 800ml hot vegetable stock
- Salt & pepper to taste

Preparation

1. Add all the ingredients to the soup maker. Don't fill the soup maker above the MAX fill line or below the min line. Add more stock if needed.
2. Set on 'smooth soup' function.
3. Once the cycle is complete, season with salt & pepper, stir and transfer into bowls, then serve.

TOMATO & RED PEPPER SOUP

Serves : 4   Cook Time : 28 Mins

Ingredients

- 1 tbsp oil
- 600g tomatoes
- 1 red pepper, chopped
- 200g potatoes, chopped
- 1 onion, chopped
- 3 garlic cloves, minced
- 400ml hot chicken stock
- 1 tbsp dried basil
- 2 tbsp tomato puree
- Salt & pepper to taste

Preparation Steps

1. In a frying pan or in your soup maker, heat oil and sauté the onions, pepper and garlic, until fragrant.
2. Switch off sauté, and add all ingredients to the soup maker and stir well. Don't fill the soup maker above the MAX fill line or below the min line. Add more stock if needed.
3. Set on 'smooth soup' function .
4. Once the cycle is complete, remove lid and season with salt & pepper and stir.
5. Transfer into bowls, and serve with croutons.

PARSNIP AND CARROT SOUP

🥣 **Serves : 4**   🕐 **Cook Time : 26 Mins**

Ingredients

- 1 onion, chopped
- 1 garlic clove, minced
- 2 parsnips, chopped
- 2 carrots, chopped
- 1 tbsp oil
- 2 tbsp curry paste

- 3 tbsp freshly chopped coriander
- 150ml coconut milk
- 700ml hot chicken stock
- Salt & pepper to taste

Preparation Steps

1. In a frying pan or in your soup maker, heat oil and sauté the onions and garlic, until fragrant. Add the parsnips and carrots, cover, stir and sauté for 2 mins.

2. Add all ingredients to the soup maker. Don't fill the soup maker above the MAX fill line or below the MIN line. Add more stock if needed.

3. Select the 'smooth soup' function.

4. Once the cycle is complete, season with salt & pepper and stir. Transfer into bowls, then serve.

SPICED PARSNIP APPLE SOUP

Serves : 4   **Cook Time : 26 Mins**

Ingredients

- 1 onion, chopped
- 2 parsnips, cut into small pieces
- 2 apples, peeled, cored & sliced
- 1 red chilli, seeded & chopped
- 1 tbsp grated fresh ginger

- 1 tbsp oil
- 700ml hot chicken stock
- 1 tbsp parsley, chopped
- Salt & pepper to taste

Preparation Steps

1. In a frying pan or in your soup maker, heat oil and sauté the onions, until fragrant. Add parsnips sauté for 5 mins.

2. Add all ingredients to the soup maker. Fill with hot stock. Don't fill the soup maker above the MAX fill line or below the MIN line. Add more stock if needed.

3. Select the 'smooth soup' function.

4. Once the cycle is complete, season with salt & pepper and stir. Transfer into bowls, then serve.

LEEK AND POTATO SOUP

🥣 Serves : 4   🕐 Cook Time : 28 Mins

Ingredients

- 1 tbsp oil
- 2 leeks, sliced
- 300g potato, peeled and chopped
- 1 onion, chopped

- 2 garlic cloves , minced
- 1 litre hot vegetable stock
- Salt & pepper to taste

Preparation

1. In a frying pan, sauté the onions with oil, until fragrant.

2. Add all the ingredients to the soup maker. Don't fill the soup maker above the MAX fill line or below the min line. Add more stock if needed.

3. Set on 'smooth soup' function.

4. Once the cycle is complete, season with salt & pepper, stir and transfer into bowls, then serve.

MINESTRONE SOUP

Serves : 4 **Cook Time : 35 Mins**

Ingredients

- 1 tbsp oil
- 1 onion, chopped
- 2 carrots, chopped
- 2 celery stalks, chopped
- 400g tin chopped tomatoes
- 200g courgettes, chopped
- 80g pasta
- 1tbsp basil
- Salt & pepper to taste

Preparation Steps

1. In a frying pan or in the soup maker, heat oil and sauté the onions and celery until soft.

2. Add all the ingredients to the soup maker. Don't fill the soup maker above the MAX fill line or below the min line. Add more stock if needed.

3. Set on 'chunky soup' function.

4. Once the cycle is complete, transfer into bowls, then serve.

VEGETABLE PASTA BOWLS

Serves : 4   Cook Time : 35 Mins

Ingredients

- 50g green beans, choppen into 1-cm pieces
- 50g kidney beans
- 150g Pasta
- 1 onion, chopped
- 1 carrot, , peeled & chopped
- 1 Potato, peeled & chopped
- 1 Small courgette, peeled & chopped
- 400g tinned crushed tomatoes
- 200ml chicken or hot vegetable stock
- 2 garlic cloves, minced
- 1 tsp of each (oregano, basil & thyme)
- 2 tsp smoked Paprika
- Salt & pepper to taste

Preparation Steps

1. In a frying pan or in the soup maker, heat oil and sauté the onions and garlic until soft.
2. Add all the ingredients to the soup maker. Don't fill the soup maker above the MAX fill line or below the min line. Add more stock if needed.
3. Set on 'chunky soup' function.
4. Once the cycle is complete, transfer into bowls, then serve.

TOMATO & CHICKPEA SOUP

Serves : 4   **Cook Time : 30 Mins**

Ingredients

- 2 onions, chopped
- 400g tinned chickpeas, drained
- 400g tinned chopped tomatoes
- 800ml hot chicken stock
- 1 garlic clove, minced
- Salt & pepper to taste

- 1/2 tsp of each (oregano, basil & thyme)
- Salt & pepper to taste

Preparation Steps

1. Add all the ingredients to the soup maker and stir well. Don't fill the soup maker above the MAX fill line or below the min line. Add more stock if needed.
2. Set on 'chunky soup' function .
3. Once the cycle is complete, season with salt & pepper and stir. Transfer into bowls, and serve.

LENTIL SOUP

Serves : 4   Cook Time : 21 Mins

Ingredients

- 200g yellow /red lentils, or yellow split peas (soaked for an hour)
- 400g tinned crushed tomatoes
- 2 carrots, peeled & chopped
- 1 onion, chopped
- 2 garlic cloves, minced

- 1tsp grated fresh ginger
- 1tsp chilli powder
- 2 tsp oregano
- 300ml Water
- Salt & pepper to taste

Preparation Steps

1. Add all ingredients to the soup maker. Don't fill the soup maker above the MAX fill line or below the MIN line. Add more stock if needed.
2. Select the 'smooth soup' function.
3. Once the cycle is complete, season with salt & pepper and stir.
4. Transfer into bowls, then serve.

CHILLED TOMATO AND OLIVE SOUP

Serves : 4   **Cook Time : 35 Mins**

Ingredients

- 1 onion, chopped
- 3 garlic cloves, minced
- 2 red peppers, seeded & chopped
- 2 courgettes, chopped
- 8 basil leaves, chopped
- 11 small black olives, stoned & sliced

- 2 tbsp oil
- 1 tbsp vinegar
- 1⁄2 tsp sugar
- 400g tinned crushed tomatoes
- 700ml hot vegetable stock
- Salt & pepper to taste

Preparation Steps

1. In a frying pan or in soup maker, heat oil and sauté the onion and garlic, until soft & fragrant. Add the red pepper and courgettes, cover and sauté for 2 minutes.

2. Add all the ingredients (except olives) to the soup maker and stir well. Don't fill the soup maker above the MAX fill line or below the min line. Add more stock if needed.

3. Set on 'chunky soup' function .

4. Once the cycle is complete, add olives, season with salt & pepper and stir. Transfer into bowls, and serve.

CHILLED POTATO AND LEEK SOUP

🥣 **Serves : 6**   🕐 **Cook Time : 21 Mins**

Ingredients

- 1 onion, chopped
- 2 garlic cloves, minced
- 1 leek, chopped
- 1 potato, chopped
- 2 tbsp oil

- 150ml milk
- 600ml hot chicken stock
- 150ml single cream
- Salt & pepper to taste

Preparation Steps

1. In a frying pan or in your soup maker, heat oil and sauté the onions, garlic and leek, until fragrant.
2. Add all ingredients (except single cream) to the soup make. Don't fill the soup maker above the MAX fill line or below the MIN line. Add more stock if needed.
3. Select the 'smooth soup' function.
4. Once the cycle is complete, add single cream, season with salt & pepper and stir. Transfer into bowls, chill in fridge then serve.

CHILLED ROCKET AND WATERCRESS SOUP

Serves : 6   **Cook Time : 21 Mins**

Ingredients

- 1 onion, chopped
- 2 garlic cloves, minced
- 1 potato, chopped
- 2 bunches of watercress, chopped
- 2 tbsp oil
- 2 large handfuls rocket leaves
- 600ml milk

- 700ml vegetable or hot chicken stock
- 150ml single cream
- Salt & pepper to taste

Preparation Steps

1. In a frying pan or in your soup maker, heat oil and sauté the onions, garlic and leek, until fragrant.
2. Add all ingredients (except single cream) to the soup maker. Don't fill the soup maker above the MAX fill line or below the MIN line. Add more stock if needed.
3. Select the 'smooth soup' function.
4. Once the cycle is complete, add single cream, season with salt & pepper and stir. Transfer into bowls, then serve.

SPRING VEGETABLE SOUP

🥣 **Serves : 4**   🕐 **Cook Time : 35 Mins**

Ingredients

- 2 onions, chopped
- 500g mixed vegetables, such as carrots, courgettes, turnips, leeks
- 100g small spinach leaves
- 2 tbsp oil
- 1 tbsp mustard

- 700ml hot chicken stock
- Salt & pepper to taste

Preparation Steps

1. In a frying pan or in your soup maker, heat oil and sauté the onions, garlic and leek, until fragrant.

2. Add all ingredients to the soup maker. Don't fill the soup maker above the MAX fill line or below the MIN line. Add more stock if needed.

3. Select the 'smooth or chunky soup according to your preference ' function.

4. Once the cycle is complete, season with salt & pepper and stir. Transfer into bowls, then serve.

CELERIAC AND ONION SOUP

Serves : 4   Cook Time : 25 Mins

Ingredients

- 3 onions, chopped
- 500g celeriac, peeled & sliced
- 2 celery stalks, chopped
- 1 tbsp oil
- 2 tbsp lemon juice
- 700ml hot chicken stock
- Salt & pepper to taste

Preparation Steps

1. In a frying pan or in your soup maker, heat oil and sauté the onions, celeriac and celery, until fragrant.
2. Add all ingredients to the soup maker. Don't fill the soup maker above the MAX fill line or below the MIN line. Add more stock if needed.
3. Select the 'smooth soup' function.
4. Once the cycle is complete, season with salt & pepper and stir. Transfer into bowls, then serve.

SQUASH AND TOMATO SOUP

Serves : 4   **Cook Time : 25 Mins**

Ingredients

- 1 onion, chopped
- 400g butternut squash, peeled & cut into small cubes
- 1 potato, peeled & chopped
- 6 tomatoes, chopped
- 2 tbsp oil
- 8 basil leaves
- 2 tbsp tomato purée
- 700ml vegetable/hot chicken stock
- Salt & pepper to taste

Preparation Steps

1. In a frying pan or in your soup maker, heat oil and sauté the onions, until fragrant.
2. Add all ingredients to the soup maker. Don't fill the soup maker above the MAX fill line or below the MIN line. Add more stock if needed.
3. Select the 'smooth soup' function.
4. Once the cycle is complete, season with salt & pepper and stir. Transfer into bowls, then serve.

COURGETTE, GREEN PEPPER & TARRAGON SOUP

🍲 **Serves : 4**   🕐 **Cook Time : 35 Mins**

Ingredients

- 1 onion, chopped
- 2 green peppers, seeded & sliced
- 2 courgettes, chopped
- 2 potatoes, peeled & choppes
- Handful tarragon leaves, chopped

- 1 tbsp oil
- 900ml hot chicken stock
- Salt & pepper to taste

Preparation Steps

1. In a frying pan or in your soup maker, heat butter/oil and sauté the onions, garlic and leek, until fragrant. Add peppers and courgettes, sauté for 5 minutes.

2. Add all ingredients to the soup maker. Don't fill the soup maker above the MAX fill line or below the MIN line. Add more stock if needed.

3. Select the 'chunky soup' function.

4. Once the cycle is complete, season with salt & pepper and stir. Transfer into bowls, then serve.

KALE SOUP

Serves : 4   **Cook Time : 21 Mins**

Ingredients

- 200g kale
- 800ml hot chicken stock
- 1 potato, peeled & chopped
- 1 carrot, peeled & chopped
- 1 celery stalk, chopped
- 3 scallions, sliced
- Salt & pepper to taste

- 200g tinned crushed tomatoes
- 1 garlic clove, minced
- 100ml stock

Preparation Steps

1. Add all ingredients to the soup maker. Fill with hot stock. Don't fill the soup maker above the MAX fill line or below the MIN line. Add more stock if needed.
2. Select the 'smooth soup' function.
3. Once the cycle is complete, season with salt & pepper and stir. Transfer into bowls, then serve.

ROASTED RATATOUILLE SOUP

🍜 Serves : 4   ⏱ Cook Time : 60 Mins

Ingredients

- 1 tbsp oil
- 1 onion, halved & sliced
- 2 garlic cloves, minced
- 1 aubergine, chopped
- 1 courgette, chopped
- 1 red pepper, chopped

- 400g tin crushed tomatoes
- 2 tbsp dried basil
- 1/2 tsp balsamic vinegar
- 600ml hot chicken stock
- Salt & pepper to taste

Preparation Steps

1. Preheat oven on 200c and place all of the vegetables except tomatoes in a large sheet pan. Season with salt and pepper and coat with oil. Roast for 30 minutes. Stirring halfway through cooking time.

2. Remove from oven transfer to your soup maker along with remaining ingredients. Don't fill the soup maker above the MAX fill line or below the min line. Add more stock if needed.

3. Set on 'chunky soup' function.

4. Once the cycle is complete, season with salt & pepper, stir and transfer into bowls, then serve.

CREAM OF RADISH SOUP

Serves : 4   Cook Time : 30 Mins

Ingredients

- 1 tbsp oil
- 250g radishes, chopped
- 1 onion, chopped
- 1 garlic clove, minced
- 1 tsp grated fresh ginger
- 1 large potato, peeled & chopped

- 1 celery stick, chopped
- 800ml hot chicken stock
- 100ml milk
- Salt & pepper to taste

Preparation Steps

1. In a frying pan or in the soup maker, add oil, sauté the onions, celery and garlic, until fragrant. Add radishes and potato and continue to sauté for 4 minutes.

2. Add all ingredients to the soup maker. Don't fill the soup maker above the MAX fill line or below the min line. Add more stock if needed.

3. Set on 'smooth soup' function.

4. Once the cycle is complete, season with salt & pepper, stir and transfer into bowls, then serve.

2

Meat & Poultry soups

CREAMY BEEF & MUSHROOM SOUP

Serves : 4   **Cook Time : 40 Mins**

Ingredients

- 130g Beef rump steak, cut into thin strips
- 2 tbsp butter
- 1 onion, chopped
- 2 garlic cloves, minced
- 350g mushrooms, sliced
- 700ml beef stock
- 120ml double cream
- 1 tbsp lemon juice

Preparation Steps

1. In a frying pan or in soup maker, heat oil and sauté the beef until browned. Add the onion and garlic and sauté for 3 minutes. Add the mushrooms and sauté for 4 minutes.
2. Add all ingredients to the soup maker. Don't fill the soup maker above the MAX fill line or below the MIN line. Add more stock if needed.
3. Select the 'chunky soup' function.
4. Once the cycle is complete, season with salt & pepper and stir.
5. Transfer into bowls, then serve.

BEEF, POTATO & PEAS SOUP

Serves : 4   Cook Time : 40 Mins

Ingredients

- 250g beef stew meat , cut into thin strips
- 1 carrot , chopped
- 1 celery stalk, chopped
- 2 tbsp oil
- 1 onion, chopped
- 2 garlic cloves, minced
- 2 potatoes , cubed
- 100g frozen peas.
- 2 tbsp tomato puree
- 1 bay leaf
- 750ml beef stock
- Salt & pepper to taste

Preparation Steps

1. In a frying pan or in soup maker, heat oil and sauté the beef until browned. Add the carrot, celery, onion and garlic. Sauté for 3 minutes.

2. Add all ingredients to the soup maker. Don't fill the soup maker above the MAX fill line or below the MIN line. Add more stock if needed.

3. Select the 'chunky soup' function.

4. Once the cycle is complete, season with salt & pepper and stir.

5. Transfer into bowls, then serve.

BEEF & KALE SOUP

Serves : 4   Cook Time : 30 Mins

Ingredients

- 225g cooked beef, sliced
- 120g fresh kale leaves , torn
- 1 onion, chopped
- 2 garlic cloves, minced
- 1 tsp rosemary
- 700ml beef stock
- 1 tbsp soy sauce
- 1 tsp lemon juice
- Salt & pepper to taste

Preparation Steps

1. Add all ingredients to the soup maker. Don't fill the soup maker above the MAX fill line or below the MIN line. Add more stock if needed.
2. Select the 'chunky soup' function.
3. Once the cycle is complete, season with salt & pepper and stir.
4. Transfer into bowls, then serve.

MEATBALL SOUP

Serves : 4   **Cook Time : 40 Mins**

Ingredients

- 120g mushrooms, sliced
- 80g dried pasta
- 200g meatballs
- 1 bay leaf
- 400g tinned crushed tomatoes
- 1 onion, chopped
- 2 garlic cloves, minced
- 1 tsp Worcestershire sauce
- 800ml hot chicken stock
- 80g grated cheese
- Salt & pepper to taste

Preparation Steps

1. In a frying pan or in soup maker, heat oil and sauté the meatballs until browned.
2. Add all ingredients to the soup maker. Don't fill the soup maker above the MAX fill line or below the MIN line. Add more stock if needed.
3. Select the 'chunky soup' function.
4. Once the cycle is complete, season with salt & pepper and stir.
5. Transfer into bowls, then serve.

BEEF & LENTIL SOUP

Serves : 4   Cook Time : 40 Mins

Ingredients

- 300g hanger steak, skirt steak cut into small cubes
- 100g dried lentils, soaked for 15 minutes
- 2 potatoes, peeled & chopped
- 2 carrots, peeled & chopped
- 1 onion, chopped
- 2 garlic cloves, minced

- 1 tsp dried rosemary
- 800ml beef stock
- Salt & pepper to taste

Preparation Steps

1. In a frying pan or in soup maker, heat oil and sauté the beef until browned.

2. Add all the ingredients to the soup maker and stir well. Don't fill the soup maker above the MAX fill line or below the min line. Add more stock if needed.

3. Set on 'chunky soup' function .

4. Once the cycle is complete, season with salt & pepper and stir. Transfer into bowls, and serve.

MINCED BEEF & TOMATO SOUP

Serves : 4   Cook Time : 40 Mins

Ingredients

- 1 tbsp oil.
- 1 onion, chopped
- 2 garlic cloves, minced
- 250g lean minced beef
- 400g tinned crushed tomatoes
- 700ml beef stock
- 1 tbsp dried rosemary
- 1 tbsp dried oregano
- Salt & pepper to taste

Preparation Steps

1. In a frying pan or in soup maker, heat oil and sauté the beef, onion, and garlic for 8 minutes.
2. Add all the ingredients to the soup maker and stir well. Don't fill the soup maker above the MAX fill line or below the min line. Add more stock if needed.
3. Set on 'chunky soup' function .
4. Once the cycle is complete, season with salt & pepper and stir. Transfer into bowls, and serve.

MINCED BEEF & BEANS SOUP

Serves : 4   **Cook Time : 40 Mins**

Ingredients

- 200g lean minced beef
- 1 onion, chopped
- 2 garlic cloves, minced
- 1 carrot, chopped
- 400g tinned crushed tomatoes
- 240ml hot chicken stock
- 1 tsp dried basil

- 200g tinned cannellini beans, rinsed & drained
- Salt & pepper to taste

Preparation Steps

1. In a frying pan or in soup maker, heat oil and sauté the beef, onion, carrot and garlic for 6 minutes.
2. Add all the ingredients to the soup maker and stir well. Don't fill the soup maker above the MAX fill line or below the min line. Add more stock if needed.
3. Set on 'chunky soup' function .
4. Once the cycle is complete, season with salt & pepper and stir. Transfer into bowls, and serve.

LAMB & MUSHROOM SOUP

Serves : 4   **Cook Time : 40 Mins**

Ingredients

- 200g lamb neck fillet, trimmed of fat and cut into small pieces
- 1 tbsp oil
- 225g fresh mushrooms , sliced
- 1 onion, chopped
- 2 garlic cloves, minced
- 1 green chili, chopped
- 1 tsp dried thyme

- 700ml hot chicken stock
- 1 tbsp lemon juice – 1 tbsp.
- Salt & pepper to taste

Preparation Steps

1. In a frying pan or in soup maker, heat oil and sauté the lamb until browned.
2. Add all the ingredients to the soup maker and stir well. Don't fill the soup maker above the MAX fill line or below the min line. Add more stock if needed.
3. Set on 'chunky soup' function .
4. Once the cycle is complete, season with salt & pepper and stir. Transfer into bowls, and serve.

LAMB & RICE SOUP

Serves : 4   Cook Time : 30 Mins

Ingredients

- 350g cooked lamb, cut into bite-sized pieces
- 180g cooked rice
- 1 onion, chopped
- 2 garlic cloves, minced
- 4 tbsp tomato puree
- 800ml beef stock
- Salt & pepper to taste

Preparation Steps

1. Add all the ingredients to the soup maker and stir well. Don't fill the soup maker above the MAX fill line or below the min line. Add more stock if needed.
2. Set on 'chunky soup' function .
3. Once the cycle is complete, season with salt & pepper and stir. Transfer into bowls, and serve.

BEEF STIR FRY SOUP

Serves : 4   Cook Time : 45 Mins

Ingredients

- 200g hanger steak, skirt steak cut into small cubes
- 600g mixed stir fry vegetables
- 2 garlic cloves, minced
- Salt & pepper to taste

- 1 tsp grated fresh ginger
- 1 litre beef stock
- Salt & pepper to taste
- 1 tsp soy sauce
- 2 tbsp oil

Preparation Steps

1. In a frying pan or in soup maker, heat oil and sauté the beef until browned.
2. Add all the ingredients to the soup maker and stir well. Don't fill the soup maker above the MAX fill line or below the min line. Add more stock if needed.
3. Set on 'chunky soup' function .
4. Once the cycle is complete, season with salt & pepper and stir. Transfer into bowls, and serve.

CHEESY & CREAMY CHICKEN SOUP

Serves : 4   Cook Time : 35 Mins

Ingredients

- 1 tbsp butter
- 4 tomatoes, chopped
- 1 jalapeño pepper, seeded & chopped
- 1 tsp taco seasoning
- 500ml hot chicken stock
- 120g cream cheese, softened
- 250g shredded cooked chicken
- 60ml double cream
- Salt & pepper to taste

Preparation Steps

1. In a frying pan or in the soup maker, heat butter and sauté the pepper and tomatoes for 3 minutes.
2. Add all the ingredients to the soup maker and stir. Don't fill the soup maker above the MAX fill line or below the min line. Add more stock if needed.
3. Set on 'chunky soup' function.
4. Once the cycle is complete, season with salt & pepper, stir and transfer into bowls, then serve.

CHICKEN NOODLE SOUP

◡ **Serves : 4**   🕐 **Cook Time : 40 Mins**

Ingredients

- 1 onion, peeled, cut in 2.5-cm pieces
- 2 celery stalks , cut in 2.5-cm pieces
- 2 carrots, peeled, cut in 2.5-cm pieces
- 850ml hot chicken stock
- 1/4 tsb dried thyme

- 150g uncooked chicken, cut in 2.5-cm pieces
- 60g dry egg noodles
- Salt & pepper to taste

Preparation Steps

1. In a frying pan or in soup maker, heat oil and sauté the onions, celery and carrots, until fragrant.
2. Add all the ingredients to the soup maker and stir well. Don't fill the soup maker above the MAX fill line or below the MIN line. Add more stock if needed.
3. Select the 'chunky soup' function.
4. When time is up, serve immediately.

TURKEY AND SWEETCORN CHOWDER

🥣 **Serves : 4**   🕐 **Cook Time : 35 Mins**

Ingredients

- 1 onion, chopped
- 1 celery stalk, chopped
- 1 potato, peeled and cut into small pieces
- 150g sweetcorn kernels
- 150g turkey breast meat
- 1 tbsp oil

- 1 tsp butter
- 400ml milk
- 300ml hot chicken stock
- 4 tbsp double cream
- Salt & pepper to taste

Preparation Steps

1. In a frying pan or in the soup maker, sauté the onions and turkey meat pieces, until golden.

2. Add all ingredients (except double cream) to the soup maker. Don't fill the soup maker above the MAX fill line or below the min line. Add more stock if needed.

3. Set on 'smooth soup' function.

4. Once the cycle is complete, season with salt & pepper, add double cream, stir and transfer into bowls, then serve.

TURKEY SOUP WITH RICE NOODLES

🥣 **Serves : 4**   🕐 **Cook Time : 30 Mins**

Ingredients

- 4 scallions, thinly sliced
- 1 leek, thinly sliced
- 1 carrot, thinly sliced
- 2 garlic cloves, minced
- 100g shredded cabbage
- 1 tsp grated fresh ginger
- Salt & pepper to taste

- 300g boneless turkey, cut into small pieces
- 1 tbsp olive oil
- 2 tsp chilli paste
- 1 tbsp fish sauce
- 900ml hot chicken stock
- 300g dry rice noodles

Preparation Steps

1. Add all the ingredients to the soup maker and stir. Don't fill the soup maker above the MAX fill line or below the min line. Add more stock if needed.
2. Set on 'chunky soup' function.
3. Once the cycle is complete, season with salt & pepper, stir and transfer into bowls, then serve.

CHICKEN COCONUT SOUP

🥣 **Serves : 4**   🕐 **Cook Time : 30 Mins**

Ingredients

- 500ml hot chicken stock
- 500ml unsweetened coconut milk
- 1 tbsp fish sauce
- 1 tbsp soy sauce
- 1 tbsp lemon juice

- 2 garlic cloves, minced
- 1 tsp ground ginger
- 180g boneless chicken breasts, cut into bite-sized pieces
- 5 basil leaves, chopped
- Salt & pepper to taste

Preparation Steps

1. Add all the ingredients to the soup maker and stir. Don't fill the soup maker above the MAX fill line or below the min line. Add more stock if needed.
2. Set on 'chunky soup' function.
3. Once the cycle is complete, season with salt & pepper, stir and transfer into bowls, then serve.

CHICKEN TARRAGON SOUP

🥣 **Serves : 4**   🕐 **Cook Time : 30 Mins**

Ingredients

- 1 tbsp oil
- 1 onion, chopped2 garlic cloves, minced
- 150g cooked chicken, shredded

- 350ml water/stock
- 2 tbsp tarragon
- 180ml double cream
- Salt & pepper to taste

Preparation Steps

1. In a frying pan or in the soup maker, heat oil, sauté the onion, until fragrant. Add the garlic and stir. Cook for a minute.

2. Add all the ingredients (except the double cream) to the soup maker and stir. Don't fill the soup maker above the MAX fill line or below the min line. Add more stock if needed.

3. Select the 'smooth soup' function.

4. Once the cycle is complete, add the double cream, season with salt & pepper, add the cheese and stir.

5. Transfer into bowls, then serve.

CHICKEN & CHILE SOUP

Serves : 4   **Cook Time : 30 Mins**

Ingredients

- 150g cooked chicken, shredded
- 1 onion, chopped
- 125g tin chopped green chiles
- 3 tomatoes, chopped
- 500ml hot chicken stock
- 1 tsp ground cumin

- 1 tsp ground coriander
- 60ml double cream
- 2 garlic cloves, minced
- 1 Jalapeño pepper, seeded and chopped
- Salt & pepper to taste

Preparation Steps

1. Add all the ingredients to the soup maker and stir to make sure nothing is stuck to the bottom. Don't fill the soup maker above the MAX fill line or below the min line. Add more stock if needed.
2. Select the 'chunky soup' function.
3. Once the cycle is complete, season with salt & pepper, and stir.
4. Transfer into bowls, then serve.

CHICKEN TIKKA MASALA SOUP

🥣 Serves : 4   🕐 Cook Time : 40 Mins

Ingredients

- 4 cooked chicken breasts, (shredded)
- 1 tbsp olive oil
- 1 onion, (diced)
- 3 garlic cloves, (minced)
- 4 tbsp chicken tikka powder
- 1 tsp. ground ginger
- 300g tomato pure
- 800ml hot chicken stock
- 150ml double cream

Preparation Steps

1. In a frying pan or in your soup maker, heat the oil and sauté the onions for a couple of minutes, add the garlic and sauté for another minute.

2. Add the chicken tikka powder & ginger and sauté for another minute. Deglaze with little stock and scrape off any stuck spices.

3. Add the cooked chicken, tomato pure and the onion and spices mixture to the soup maker.

4. Add the stock up to the MAX line, stir and press 'chunky soup' function. Don't fill the soup maker above the max fill line.

5. Once the cycle is complete, lift the lid off and season with salt & pepper, stir in the cream. transfer into bowls and serve.

CHICKEN & COURGETTE SOUP

🥣 **Serves : 4**   🕐 **Cook Time : 40 Mins**

Ingredients

- 1 tbsp oil
- 1 carrot, chopped
- 1 courgette , chopped
- 1 onion, chopped
- 1 celery stalk, chopped
- 1 tbsp of each (rosemary and thyme)

- 1 litre hot chicken stock
- 1 skinless, boneless chicken breast, chopped
- 1 tbsp fresh lemon juice
- Salt & pepper to taste

Preparation Steps

1. In a frying pan or in soup maker, heat oil and sauté the onions, carrot and garlic, until soft & fragrant. Add chicken and sauté for 3 minutes.

2. Add all the ingredients to the soup maker and stir well. Don't fill the soup maker above the MAX fill line or below the min line. Add more stock if needed.

3. Set on 'chunky soup' function .

4. Once the cycle is complete, season with salt & pepper and stir. Transfer into bowls, and serve.

CREAMY CHICKEN & CAULIFLOWER SOUP

🍲 **Serves : 4**   🕐 **Cook Time : 35 Mins**

Ingredients

- 1 carrot, chopped
- 1 onion, chopped
- 1 celery stalk, chopped
- 1 garlic clove, minced
- 150g cauliflower, chopped
- 1 skinless, boneless chicken breast, chopped

- 1 tbsp dried parsley
- 700ml hot chicken stock
- 120ml double cream
- 1 tbsp butter
- Salt & pepper to taste

Preparation Steps

1. In a frying pan or in soup maker, heat butter and sauté the onions, celery, carrots and garlic, until soft & fragrant.
2. Add all the ingredients to the soup maker and stir well. Don't fill the soup maker above the MAX fill line or below the min line. Add more stock if needed.
3. Set on 'chunky soup' function .
4. Once the cycle is complete, season with salt & pepper and stir. Transfer into bowls, and serve.

CHICKEN, CARROT & POTATO SOUP

Serves : 4   **Cook Time : 30 Mins**

Ingredients

- 1 boneless, skinless chicken breast, cut into small pieces
- 3 potatoes, chopped
- 2 celery stalks, chopped
- 1 carrot, chopped
- 1 chilli, (chopped)
- ½ tsp. ground cumin
- 800ml chicken broth
- 120ml double cream
- Salt & pepper to taste

Preparation Steps

1. Add all the ingredients (except double cream) to the soup maker and stir. Don't fill the soup maker above the MAX fill line or below the min line. Add more stock if needed.
2. Set on 'chunky soup' function .
3. Once the cycle is complete, add double cream, season with salt & pepper and stir. Transfer into bowls, and serve

CHICKEN & MUSHROOM SOUP

Serves : 4   **Cook Time : 35 Mins**

Ingredients

- 1 tbsp oil
- 2 skinless/boneless chicken breasts, chopped
- 250g mushrooms, sliced
- 1 onion, chopped
- 1 garlic clove, minced
- 1 carrot, peeled & chopped
- 1 celery stalk, chopped
- 800ml hot chicken stock
- 100ml milk
- 1 tsp Worcestershire sauce
- 1 tsp dried thyme
- Salt & pepper to taste

Preparation Steps

1. In a frying pan or in your soup maker, heat the oil and Add the chicken and sauté until golden. Sauté the onions and garlic until softened.

2. Add the carrot, mushrooms and celery and sauté for 6 minutes before adding the mushrooms.

3. Add all the ingredients to the soup maker (except cream) and stir well. Don't fill the soup maker above the MAX fill line or below the min line. Add more water if needed.

4. Set on 'smooth soup' function .

5. Once the cycle is complete, season with salt & pepper, add cream and stir. Transfer into bowls, and serve.

CHICKEN & SWEETCORN CHOWDER

Serves : 4   **Cook Time : 40 Mins**

Ingredients

- 1 tbsp oil
- 2 skinless, boneless chicken breasts, chopped
- 300g potato, peeled & chopped
- 150ml milk
- 1 onion, chopped
- 2 celery stalks, chopped
- 260g tin drained sweetcorn

- 1 bay leaf
- 2 tsp paprika
- 1 tsp dried thyme
- 700ml hot chicken stock
- Salt & pepper to taste

Preparation Steps

1. In a frying pan or in your soup maker, heat the oil and Add the chicken and sauté until golden. Sauté the onions for a couple of minutes, add the garlic and sauté for another minute.

2. Add all the ingredients to the soup maker. Don't fill the soup maker above the MAX fill line or below the min line. Add more stock if needed.

3. Set on 'chunky soup' function.

4. Once the cycle is complete, remove the bay leaf. Pour half of the soup in to a blender and blend until smooth, then transfer back in to the soup maker and

5. season with salt & pepper, transfer into bowls, then serve.

CHICKEN & VEGETABLE SOUP

Serves : 4   **Cook Time : 30 Mins**

Ingredients

- 1 tbsp oil
- 2 skinless, boneless chicken breasts, chopped
- 2 tbsp dried thyme
- 2 garlic cloves, minced
- 150g scallions, chopped
- 140g mushrooms, sliced
- Salt & pepper to taste

- 1 tsp grated fresh ginger
- 1 bell pepper, deseeded & chopped
- 250g potato, peeled & chopped
- 900ml hot chicken stock

Preparation Steps

1. In a frying pan or in soup maker, heat oil and sauté the onions, ginger, mushroom and garlic, until soft & fragrant.
2. Add all the ingredients to the soup maker and stir well. Don't fill the soup maker above the MAX fill line or below the min line. Add more stock if needed.
3. Set on 'smooth soup' function .
4. Once the cycle is complete, season with salt & pepper and stir. Transfer into bowls, and serve.

ITALIAN CHICKEN & TOMATO SOUP

🥣 **Serves : 4** 🕐 **Cook Time : 40 Mins**

Ingredients

- 1 tbsp oil
- 1 onion, chopped
- 1 garlic clove, minced
- 250g chicken breasts, chopped
- 1 bell pepper, deseeded & chopped
- 1 celery stalk, chopped
- 400g tin crushed tomatoes
- 160g runner beans, chopped
- 2 tbsp chopped fresh rosemary
- 500ml hot chicken stock
- Salt & pepper to taste

Preparation Steps

1. In a frying pan or in your soup maker, sauté the onions, peppers, celery and chicken, until golden. the chicken until golden brown.
2. Add all the ingredients to the soup maker. Don't fill the soup maker above the MAX fill line or below the min line. Add more stock if needed.
3. Set on 'chunky soup' function.
4. Once the cycle is complete, season with salt & pepper, stir and transfer into bowls, then serve.

CHICKEN & CHORIZO SOUP

🥣 **Serves : 4**   🕐 **Cook Time : 40 Mins**

Ingredients

- 1 tbsp oil
- 1 chicken breast, chopped
- 2 onion, chopped
- 1 garlic clove, minced
- 40g chorizo, chopped

- 300g sweet potato, peeled & chopped
- 400g tin crushed tomatoes
- 600ml water
- Salt & pepper to taste

Preparation Steps

1. In a frying pan or in your soup maker, sauté the onions and chicken, until golden.
2. Add all the ingredients to the soup maker. Don't fill the soup maker above the MAX fill line or below the min line. Add more stock if needed.
3. Set on 'chunky soup' function.
4. Once the cycle is complete, season with salt & pepper, stir and transfer into bowls, then serve.

CHICKEN, GINGER & LEMON SOUP

Serves : 4   **Cook Time : 40 Mins**

Ingredients

- 1 tbsp oil
- 2 cooked chicken breast, chopped
- 4 scallions, trimmed & chopped
- 200g Butternut squash, peeled & chopped
- 3 garlic cloves, minced
- 1tsp grated fresh ginger
- 1 litre hot chicken stock

- 200g button mushrooms, sliced
- 1 & 1/2 tsp turmeric
- 2 tbsp lemon juice
- 1 tsp ground coriander
- 1/8 tsp sugar
- Salt & pepper to taste

Preparation Steps

1. In a frying pan or in your soup maker, saute the scallions until fragrant. Add Butternut and chicken and cook for 6 minutes.
2. Add all the ingredients (except lemon juice) to the soup maker. Don't fill the soup maker above the MAX fill line or below the min line. Add more stock if needed.
3. Set on 'chunky soup' function.
4. Once the cycle is complete, add lemon juice, season with salt & pepper, stir and transfer into bowls, then serve.

THAI CHICKEN AND RED CHILLI SOUP

Serves : 2   Cook Time : 30 Mins

Ingredients

- 2 shallots, chopped
- 2 celery stalks, chopped
- 150g mushrooms, chopped
- 300g boneless fresh chicken
- 1 tbsp oil

- 2 tbsp Thai chilli paste
- 2 tbsp fish sauce
- 100g spinach leaves
- 700ml hot chicken stock
- Salt & pepper to taste

Preparation Steps

1. Add all the ingredients to the soup maker. Don't fill the soup maker above the MAX fill line or below the min line. Add more stock if needed.
2. Set on 'chunky soup' function.
3. Once the cycle is complete, season with salt & pepper, stir and transfer into bowls, then serve.

LEMON CHICKEN AND MUSHROOM SOUP

Serves : 2   **Cook Time : 21 Mins**

Ingredients

- 2 shallots, chopped
- 2 celery stalks, chopped
- 150g mushrooms, chopped
- 300g boneless chicken, cut into small pieces
- 1 lemon, juice & zest

- 1 tbsp oil
- 100g spinach leaves
- 700ml hot chicken stock
- Salt & pepper to taste

Preparation Steps

1. Add all the ingredients to the soup maker. Don't fill the soup maker above the MAX fill line or below the min line. Add more stock if needed.
2. Set on 'smooth soup' function.
3. Once the cycle is complete, season with salt & pepper, stir and transfer into bowls, then serve.

GREEK LEMON CHICKEN

🥣 Serves : 4   🕐 Cook Time : 30 Mins

Ingredients

- 1 chicken breast, boneless, skinless & cut into cubes
- 1 onion, chopped
- 1 red Pepper, chopped
- 2 tsp chives, chopped
- 3 garlic cloves
- 150ml Water

- 3 tbsp double cream
- 1 Lemon (zest and juice)
- 150g couscous
- 150g Feta cheese
- Salt & pepper to taste

Preparation Steps

1. Add all the ingredients (except double cream & feta cheese) to the soup maker. Don't fill the soup maker above the MAX fill line or below the min line. Add more stock if needed.

2. Set on 'Chunky soup' function.

3. Once the cycle is complete, add double cream and feta cheese, season with salt & pepper, stir and transfer into bowls, then serve.

CREAMY CHICKEN & POTATO SOUP

Serves : 2   Cook Time : 21 Mins

Ingredients

- 200g shredded cooked chicken
- 2 garlic cloves, minced
- 1 onion, chopped
- 200g potatoes, chopped
- 500ml hot chicken stock
- 2 tbsp double cream
- Salt & pepper to taste

Preparation Steps

1. Add all the ingredients (except double cream) to the soup maker. Don't fill the soup maker above the MAX fill line or below the min line. Add more stock if needed.
2. Set on 'smooth soup' function.
3. Once the cycle is complete, season with salt & pepper, stir and transfer into bowls, then serve.

3

Seafood soups

SMOKED SALMON SOUP

🥣 **Serves : 4**   🕐 **Cook Time : 30 Mins**

Ingredients

- 2 tbsp butter
- 1 celery stalk, chopped
- 1 onion, chopped
- Salt & pepper to taste

- 1 garlic clove, minced
- 380ml hot chicken stock
- 1 tbsp tomato puree
- cream cheese, softened
- Smoked salmon, chopped

Preparation Steps

1. In a frying pan or in your soup maker, heat butter and sauté celery, onion & salt for 5 mins. Add the garlic & sauté for 1 min.

2. Add all ingredients (except cream cheese & smoked salmon) to the soup maker. Don't fill the soup maker above the MAX fill line or below the MIN line. Add more stock if needed.

3. Select the 'smooth soup' function.

4. Once the cycle is complete, add cream cheese and smoked salmon, season with salt & pepper and stir. Transfer into bowls, then serve.

CREAMY SALMON SOUP

Serves : 4   Cook Time : 30 Mins

Ingredients

- 240ml hot chicken stock
- 1 tbsp plain flour
- 500ml milk
- 650g tinned salmon, bones removed
- Salt & pepper to taste

Preparation Steps

1. In a bowl, add stock and flour and mix. Add to the soup maker.

2. Add all remaining ingredients to the soup maker and stir to make sure nothing is stuck to the bottom. Don't fill the soup maker above the MAX fill line or below the MIN line. Add more stock if needed.

3. Select the 'chunky soup' function.

4. Once the cycle is complete, season with salt & pepper, and stir.

5. Transfer into bowls, then serve.

SEA-FISH SOUP

Serves : 3   **Cook Time : 40 Mins**

Ingredients

- 1 onion, finely chopped
- 2 garlic cloves, minced
- 1 carrot, cut into small pieces
- 200g cooked smoked white fish, flaked & bones removed
- 1 tbsp oil
- 400g tin crushed tomatoes
- 2 tbsp tomato purée

- 1 tbsp lemon juice
- 2 tbsp fish sauce
- 700ml hot chicken stock
- 100g cooked peeled prawns
- Salt and pepper to taste

Preparation Steps

1. In a frying pan or in the soup maker, heat oil, sauté the onion, garlic until fragrant.

2. Add all the remaining ingredients (except fish & prawns) to the soup maker and stir to make sure nothing is stuck to the bottom. Don't fill the soup maker above the MAX fill line or below the MIN line. Add more stock if needed.

3. Select the 'chunky soup' function.

4. Open lid, add prawns and fish. Stir, let set 3 minutes. Serve.

PORTUGUESE FISH SOUP

🥣 Serves : 3   🕐 Cook Time : 30 Mins

Ingredients

- 1 large carrot, peeled & chopped
- 2 potatoes, peeled & chopped
- 100g white fish, chopped
- 100g clams
- 150g Prawns
- 400g tinned crushed tomatoes
- 4 garlic cloves, minced
- 1tsp English mustard
- 2 tsp smoked paprika
- 180ml Water
- Salt & Pepper

Preparation Steps

1. Add all the ingredients to the soup maker and stir to make sure nothing is stuck to the bottom. Don't fill the soup maker above the MAX fill line or below the MIN line. Add more stock if needed.
2. Select the 'chunky soup' function.
3. Once the cycle is complete, season with salt & pepper, and stir.
4. Transfer into bowls, then serve.

FISH CURRY SOUP

Serves : 4   **Cook Time : 40 Mins**

Ingredients

- 1 tbsp oil
- 250g fish fillets
- 2 onions, chopped
- 3 garlic cloves, minced
- 1 litre hot fish stock

- 1⁄2 tsp fennel seeds
- 1⁄2 tsp cumin seeds
- 1⁄2 tsp turmeric
- 1 tsp garam masala
- 1 tbsp balsamic vinegar
- 400g tinned crushed tomatoes

Preparation Steps

1. In a frying pan or in the soup maker, heat oil, sauté the onion, until fragrant. Add the garlic and stir. Add the spices and stir. Sauté for a minute.

2. Add all the ingredients to the soup maker and stir to make sure nothing is stuck to the bottom. Don't fill the soup maker above the MAX fill line or below the MIN line. Add more stock if needed.

3. Select the 'chunky soup' function.

4. Once the cycle is complete, season with salt & pepper, and stir.

5. Transfer into bowls, then serve.

THAI CURRY SOUP

🥣 **Serves : 4**   🕐 **Cook Time : 50 Mins**

Ingredients

- 240g cauliflower florets
- 250g fish fillets, chopped
- 200ml coconut milk
- 1 garlic clove, minced
- 750ml hot chicken stock
- 2 tsp grated fresh ginger

- 200g courgette, grated
- ¼ tsp turmeric
- 1 onion, thinly sliced
- 1 tsp lemon juice
- Salt & pepper to taste

Preparation Steps

1. Add cauliflower, milk and water to the soup maker and stir to make sure nothing is stuck to the bottom. Don't fill the soup maker above the MAX fill line or below the MIN line. Add more stock if needed.

2. Select the 'smooth soup' function.

3. Once the cycle is complete, add all remaining ingredients, season with salt & pepper and stir.

4. Select the 'chunky soup' function.

5. Once the cycle is complete, transfer into bowls, then serve.

TUNA TOFU SOUP

🥣 **Serves : 4**   🕐 **Cook Time : 30 Mins**

Ingredients

- 200g tofu, chopped
- 140g tin tuna in salted water drained
- 100g scallions, trimmed & sliced
- 2 tbsp miso paste
- 1.2 litre hot chicken stock
- 1 tbsp soy sauce

Preparation Steps

1. Add all the ingredients to the soup maker and stir to make sure nothing is stuck to the bottom. Don't fill the soup maker above the MAX fill line or below the MIN line. Add more stock if needed.
2. Select the 'chunky soup' function.
3. Once the cycle is complete, season with salt & pepper, and stir.
4. Transfer into bowls, then serve.

HERBED SALMON SOUP

🥣 **Serves : 4**   🕐 **Cook Time : 40 Mins**

Ingredients

- 1 tbsp oil
- 1 onion, chopped
- 1 garlic clove, minced
- 700ml hot chicken stock
- 400g boneless salmon fillet , cubed
- 1 tbsp soy sauce
- 1 tbsp lemon juice
- Salt & pepper to taste

Preparation Steps

1. In a frying pan or in the soup maker, heat oil, sauté the onion, until fragrant. Add the garlic and sauté for a minute.

2. Add all the ingredients to the soup maker and stir to make sure nothing is stuck to the bottom. Don't fill the soup maker above the MAX fill line or below the MIN line. Add more stock if needed.

3. Select the 'chunky soup' function.

4. Once the cycle is complete, season with salt & pepper, and stir.

5. Transfer into bowls, then serve.

SALMON AND POTATO SOUP

🥣 **Serves : 4**   🕐 **Cook Time : 40 Mins**

Ingredients

- 1 tbsp butter
- 1 onion, chopped
- 2 celery stalk, chopped
- 1 tsp garlic powder
- 1 potato, peeled chopped
- 1 carrots, peeled & chopped
- 500ml hot chicken stock
- 225g fresh or tinned salmon
- 50g grated cheddar cheese
- 60ml evaporated milk
- Salt and pepper to taste

Preparation Steps

1. In a frying pan or in the soup maker, heat butter, sauté the onion and celery until fragrant. Add potatoes and carrots, stock and cook for 4 mins.

2. Add all the ingredients (except salmon, cheese and evaporated) to the soup maker and stir to make sure nothing is stuck to the bottom. Don't fill the soup maker above the MAX fill line or below the MIN line. Add more stock if needed.

3. Transfer the onion mixture into a Soup Maker.

4. Select the 'chunky soup' function. In the last 10 mins add salmon, cheese and evaporated milk.

5. Once the cycle is complete, season with salt & pepper, and stir.

6. Transfer into bowls, then serve.

SALMON, MUSHROOM & CABBAGE SOUP

Serves : 4   Cook Time : 40 Mins

Ingredients

- 1 tbsp oil.
- 1 onion, chopped
- 150g cabbage , chopped
- 100g fresh mushrooms, sliced
- 700ml hot chicken stock
- 200g salmon fillets, boneless & cubed
- 1 tbsp fresh lemon juice
- Salt and pepper to taste

Preparation Steps

1. In a frying pan or in the soup maker, heat oil, sauté the onion, until fragrant. Add cabbage and mushrooms and sauté for 6 mins.

2. Add all the ingredients to the soup maker and stir to make sure nothing is stuck to the bottom. Don't fill the soup maker above the MAX fill line or below the MIN line. Add more stock if needed.

3. Select the 'chunky soup' function.

4. Once the cycle is complete, season with salt & pepper, and stir.

5. Transfer into bowls, then serve.

CULLEN SKINK

Serves : 3   Cook Time : 21 Mins

Ingredients

- 300g cooked Haddock
- 100g onion, (chopped)
- 1 garlic clove, (minced)
- 400g potatoes, (peeled & chopped)
- 600ml milk
- 200ml hot fish stock
- Salt & pepper to taste

Preparation Steps

1. Add all ingredients to the soup maker. Don't fill the soup maker above the MAX fill line or below the MIN line. Add more stock if needed.
2. Select the 'smooth soup' function.
3. Once the cycle is complete, season with salt & pepper and stir. Transfer into bowls, then serve.

MEXICAN SEAFOOD SOUP

Serves : 4   Cook Time : 40 Mins

Ingredients

- 1 tbsp oil
- 1 onion, chopped
- 1 carrot, chopped
- 2 celery stalks, chopped
- 300g tin corn kernels, drained
- 200g tin tomato sauce
- 1 litre hot chicken stock

- 500g thawed seafood mix
- ½ tsp. chili powder
- ½ tsp. oregano
- ½ tsp. cumin
- ½ tsp. garlic powder
- Salt & pepper to taste

Preparation Steps

1. In a frying pan or in soup maker, heat oil and saute the onion, celery, and carrot, until soft & fragrant.
2. Add all the ingredients to the soup maker and stir well. Don't fill the soup maker above the MAX fill line or below the min line. Add more stock if needed.
3. Set on 'chunky soup' function .
4. Once the cycle is complete, season with salt & pepper and stir. Transfer into bowls, and serve.

PRAWN SOUP

Serves : 4 **Cook Time : 30 Mins**

Ingredients

- 1 bunch scallions
- 4 tomatoes, chopped
- 1 tbsp oil
- Pinch of saffron
- 1 tbsp lemon juice

- 700ml hot chicken stock
- 2 tbsp fish sauce
- 300g prawns, cooked & peeled
- Salt & pepper to taste

Preparation Steps

1. In a frying pan or in the soup maker, heat oil, sauté the onion, until fragrant. Add the spices and stir. Cook for a minute.

2. Add all the ingredients (except prawns) to the soup maker and stir to make sure nothing is stuck to the bottom. Don't fill the soup maker above the MAX fill line or below the MIN line. Add more stock if needed.

3. Select the 'smooth soup' function.

4. Add the prawns and let set for 3 minutes.

5. Transfer into bowls, then serve.

PRAWN AND TOMATO SOUP

🥣 Serves : 4   🕐 Cook Time : 40 Mins

Ingredients

- 6 scallions, sliced
- 400g tinned crushed tomatoes
- 1 tbsp oil
- 1 tbsp lemon juice
- 2 tbsp fish sauce

- 700ml hot fish stock
- 300g prawns, peeled
- Salt & pepper to taste

Preparation Steps

1. In a frying pan or in soup maker, heat oil and saute the scallions until sfragrant.
2. Add all the ingredients to the soup maker and stir well. Don't fill the soup maker above the MAX fill line or below the MIN line. Add more stock if needed.
3. Set on 'chunky soup' function .
4. Once the cycle is complete, season with salt & pepper and stir. Transfer into bowls, and serve.

PORTUGUESE SEAFOOD SOUP

🥣 **Serves : 4**   🕐 **Cook Time : 30 Mins**

Ingredients

- 1 large carrot, peeled & chopped
- 2 medium potatoes, peeled & chopped
- 1 red pepper, chopped
- 100g white fish, diced
- 100g clams

- 100g prawns
- 400g tin crushed tomatoes
- 2 garlic clove, minced
- 1 tsp. mustard
- 2 tsp. smoked paprika
- 200ml Water
- Salt & Pepper

Preparation Steps

1. Add all ingredients to the soup maker and stir well. Don't fill the soup maker above the MAX fill line or below the MIN line. Add more water if needed.
2. Select the 'chunky soup' function.
3. Once the cycle is complete, season with salt & pepper and stir. Transfer into bowls, then serve.

SALMON AND SWEETCORN CHOWDER

Serves : 4　　**Cook Time : 40 Mins**

Ingredients

- 1 onion, chopped
- 1 potato, peeled & chopped into small pieces
- 2 tomatoes, chopped
- 150g fresh or frozen corn kernels
- 200g salmon, boneless & cut into chunks
- 1 tbsp oil

- 1 tsp butter
- 2 tsp plain flour
- 400ml milk
- 300ml hot chicken stock
- Salt & pepper to taste

Preparation Steps

1. In a frying pan or in your soup maker, heat butter and sauté the onions, until fragrant. Add the potato sauté for 3 mins.

2. Add all the ingredients to the soup maker and stir to make sure nothing is stuck to the bottom. Don't fill the soup maker above the MAX fill line or below the MIN line. Add more stock if needed.

3. Select the 'chunky soup' function.

4. Once the cycle is complete, season with salt & pepper and stir.

5. Transfer into bowls, then serve.

SALMON AND COCONUT SOUP

🥣 **Serves : 4**   🕐 **Cook Time : 30 Mins**

Ingredients

- 1 onion, chopped
- 2 carrots, peeled & thinly sliced
- 1 potato, peeled & chopped
- 300g salmon fillet, skinless, boneless and cut into small pieces
- 1 tbsp oil

- 200g tinned crushed tomatoes
- 400ml coconut milk
- 600ml hot chicken stock
- Salt & pepper to taste

Preparation Steps

1. In a frying pan or in your soup maker, heat butter and sauté the onions, until fragrant. Add the potato & carrots sauté for 3 mins.
2. Add all the ingredients to the soup maker and stir well. Don't fill the soup maker above the MAX fill line or below the MIN line. Add more stock if needed.
3. Select the 'smooth soup' function.
4. Once the cycle is complete, season with salt & pepper and stir. Transfer into bowls, then serve.

HADDOCK CHOWDER

🥣 **Serves : 6**   🕐 **Cook Time : 40 Mins**

Ingredients

- 2 tbsp butter
- 1 tbsp oil
- 1 medium onion, chopped
- 20g plain flour
- 400ml milk
- 400ml water
- 2 medium potatoes peeled, cut into cubes

- 100g sweetcorn kernels
- 1 medium leek, (sliced)
- 400g frozen smoked haddock fillets, (cut into large pieces)
- Salt & pepper to taste

Preparation Steps

1. In a frying pan or in soup maker, heat oil and saute the onion and garlic, until soft & fragrant.

2. Add all the ingredients to the soup maker and stir well. Don't fill the soup maker above the MAX fill line or below the min line. Add more stock if needed.

3. Select the 'chunky soup' function.

4. Once the cycle is complete, season with salt & pepper and stir.

5. Transfer into bowls, then serve.

SMOKED SALMON & RED PEPPER SOUP

🥣 Serves : 4   🕐 Cook Time : 26 Mins

Ingredients

- 3 red peppers, seeded & chopped
- 200g smoked salmon, chopped
- 1 tbsp oil
- 200g tin crushed tomatoes
- 1 tbsp lemon juice
- 700ml hot chicken stock
- Salt & pepper to taste

Preparation Steps

1. In a frying pan or in the soup maker, heat oil, sauté the red pepper, until fragrant. Add the spices and stir. Cook for a minute.

2. Add all the ingredients (except salmon) to the soup maker and stir to make sure nothing is stuck to the bottom. Don't fill the soup maker above the MAX fill line or below the MIN line. Add more stock if needed.

3. Select the 'smooth soup' function.

4. Once the cycle is complete, season with salt & pepper, add salmon and stir.

5. Transfer into bowls, then serve.

SALMON & RICE SOUP

Serves : 4   Cook Time : 30 Mins

Ingredients

- 140g cooked rice
- 350g salmon fillet, skinless & cut into small pieces
- 2 tbsp soy sauce
- 1 tbsp sesame oil
- 1 tbsp grated fresh ginger
- 700ml hot chicken stock
- 2 Scallions, chopped
- Salt & pepper to taste

Preparation Steps

1. Add all the ingredients to the soup maker and stir to make sure nothing is stuck to the bottom. Don't fill the soup maker above the MAX fill line or below the MIN line. Add more stock if needed.
2. Select the 'chunky soup' function.
3. Once the cycle is complete, season with salt & pepper, and stir.
4. Transfer into bowls, then serve.

Printed in Great Britain
by Amazon